AN
EASY-READ
FACT
BOOK

Big Trucks

Michael Jay

Franklin Watts

London   New York   Toronto   Sydney

© 1986 Franklin Watts Ltd

First published in Great Britain
    1986 by
Franklin Watts Ltd
12a Golden Square
London W1

First published in the USA by
Franklin Watts Inc.
387 Park Avenue South
New York
N.Y. 10016

UK ISBN: 0 86313 360 6
US ISBN: 0-531-10163-0
Library of Congress Catalog Card
    Number: 85-51598

Designed and produced by
David Jefferis

Illustrations and photographs by
Robert Burns/Drawing Attention
Hayward Art Group
David Jefferis
Michael Roffe
Volvo

Picture research by
Penny Warne

Technical consultant
Pat Bailey M.I.M.I.
Printed in Great Britain by
Cambus Litho, East Kilbride

Big Trucks

Contents

Big rigs

Trucks are the main movers of freight in countries all over the world. No other form of cargo transport offers the door-to-door convenience of today's trucks.

▽ Trucks like this have powerful diesel engines and can cruise at over 62.5 mph (100 km/h) when speed limits allow.

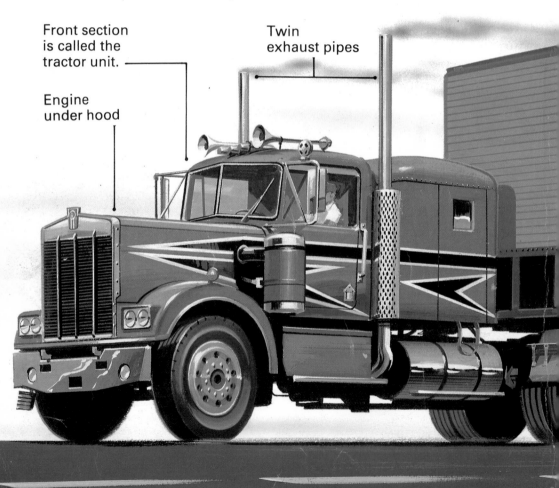

Front section is called the tractor unit.

Twin exhaust pipes

Engine under hood

Trains, boats and planes carry lots of freight, but they need a truck at either end for almost all loading, unloading and delivery jobs.

The truck shown below is a typical long-distance hauler. The semitrailer hooks to the rear part of the diesel-engined tractor unit.

▽ The rig has 18 wheels to spread the weight of the load. Road wear is a problem for all big trucks; spreading the load reduces the damage to the road surface.

Container, mounted on a semitrailer. "Semis" hook directly on to the rear of the tractor. Trailers have front wheels and a drawbar.

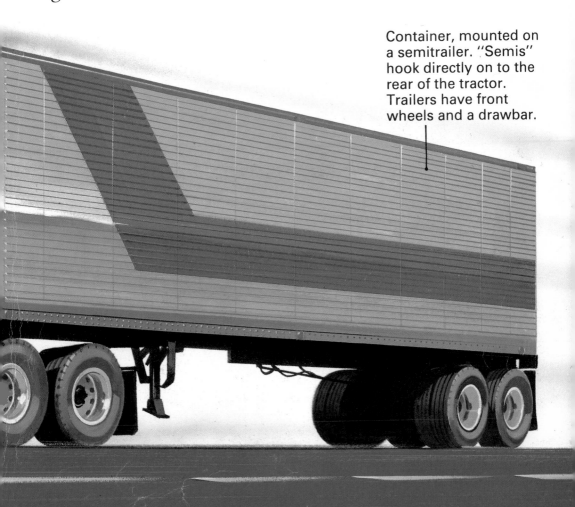

Mighty mover

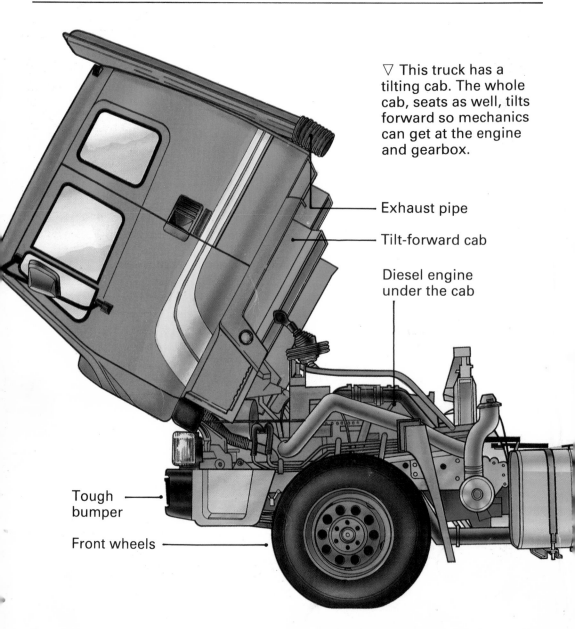

▽ This truck has a tilting cab. The whole cab, seats as well, tilts forward so mechanics can get at the engine and gearbox.

Exhaust pipe

Tilt-forward cab

Diesel engine under the cab

Tough bumper

Front wheels

The "backbone" of a big truck is the strong frame, made of steel or aluminum. Mounted up front is the engine. Wheels are mounted front and rear, with fuel tanks placed either side of the frame.

The cab is made of steel, aluminum or fiberglass. With the tilt-cab design shown here, it tilts forward to expose the engine for servicing.

△ The Mercedes-Benz on the left is a tilt-cab, with its engine under the cab. The Volvo has a conventional hood with the engine underneath.

Steel or aluminum chassis

Rear wheels, mounted in pairs either side of the chassis

Fuel tank

In the cab

△ It's a long climb up to the cab of this Volvo. Many drivers like to customise their vehicles – this big truck is a fine example!

To talk with other drivers, many truckers have CB radios. Using these, truckers can warn each other of hazards and swap other information.

Modern trucks are carefully designed to give a good driving position.

Many seats have air suspension, with power adjustment for height, back angle and distance from the steering wheel.

Steering can be power-assisted, making low-speed maneuvering easier than it used to be. The instruments are placed for easy visibility, while wide windows give a good view of the highway.

Details like these are not simply to give a trucker an easy time. Drivers spend long periods at the wheel and poor seating or badly placed controls divert attention away from the driving job. Poor window design means that the driver might not see other vehicles. So careful planning is an important safety feature of a good big truck.

For journeys with overnight stops, many cabs have sleeper sections.

△ For overnight stops, sleeper cabs like this are often used. Many have all the comforts of home, including an oven and TV.

▷ Modern cabs have the comforts of an executive car. The controls are easy to use and the seats are comfortable. Both contribute to road safety, as the driver can concentrate on the road, rather than an aching back.

Modern trucks

△ This Renault is a typical rigid design. It is a good vehicle for general deliveries.

▽ This Scammel tractor is hauling a 100-ton load, mounted on a 24-wheel trailer.

△ This ERF tanker is an articulated vehicle.

There are two main types of truck. Smaller trucks are mostly of rigid design – the vehicle is one unit, with engine, cab and load all mounted on one chassis.

Big trucks are usually articulated – they have a joint in the middle, so they can easily maneuver big loads. The tractor and semi-trailer can be unhooked, so a load can be transported while another semi is being loaded, ready for pick-up.

For really massive loads, multi-wheeled low-bed trailers like the one on the left, can be used.

11

Container trucks

Containers were first developed for ships as a standard-sized "shoebox" into which goods could be loaded. The same container may be offloaded from the ship on to a train or coupled on to a container truck. This flexibility is what has made containers so popular with shipping companies all over the world.

A typical container truck is made of three main sections. The container itself is usually 40 ft (12.19 m) long, though other sizes can be used. The normal weight limit is 33 tons (30 mt).

The second section is the semi-trailer on which the container rests. Pulling the load is the truck itself, called the tractor. Most modern vehicles are diesel powered and have tilt-cab designs.

For long distance work, many have sleeper cabs to let the drivers sleep, parked by the roadside.

△ Semitrailers have dropdown legs, used when they are un-hitched. This container has refrigeration equipment to keep its load of meat cool.

▷ This truck is an Iveco. Can you spot the custom additions, such as the airhorns and windshield visor?

▽ This picture shows the three sections of a container trucking unit.

Tractor

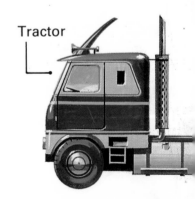

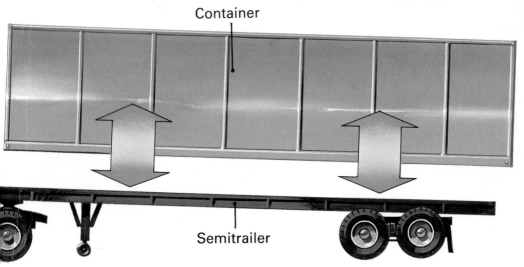

Container

Semitrailer

13

Tankers

△ The International tanker above can haul an outsize load of 20,000 gallons (77.284 l). Behind is a Mack hauling a tanker semi made by Crane Fruehauf.

Tankers carry most kinds of liquid, from gasoline and oil to milk and wine. These are simple to load and unload as they pour easily. Other liquids are not so simple. Fats need heating. If it gets cold, fat solidifies.

When carrying cold loads, such as liquid oxygen, the tanker must be insulated like a vacuum flask and carry special cooling equipment. If liquid oxygen warms up, it boils off into the

atmosphere.

Tankers can carry powder as well. Flour can be mixed with high-pressure air and blown through pipes.

Liquid sloshing around in a tanker can be a problem as a shifting load makes going around corners danger-ous. So tank insides are fitted with separate compartments and paddle-like anti-slosh baffles. These stop too much movement of the load.

△ Aircraft use huge quantities of fuel and every airport has a fleet of tanker refuelers. Behind the big tanker in this picture are smaller hydrant refuelers. These join the underground fuel lines of a big airport to the fuel tanks of the planes.

Long distance hauling

△ A Mack truck, hauling a trailer. American truckers don't have the language and customs difficulties of Europeans, but they can have paperwork when traveling between states.

Runs of several thousand miles are common in today's trucking world. Crossing international borders can be a problem, as each country has its own rules for trucking of goods.

To get round some of these problems, transcontinental trucks in Europe cary TIR plates. This sign, which means *Transportes Internationale des Routiers*, indicates that the load is checked and sealed at the country of

origin. Customs officers of various countries just need to check the driver's papers and see the load is still sealed. It is not opened until the destination is reached.

European drivers also have a tachograph in the cab. This is a meter which records speed and time on the road. Drivers are limited to eight hours at the wheel, followed by a minimum eleven hour rest period.

△ A Mercedes-Benz with a Dutch load. The truckers standing on top are spectators at a truck race. You can see what they are watching on page 30.

Roadtrain!

△ This Kenworth is a typical roadtrain. The truck is equipped with thick steel "roo bars" at the front as protection from colliding with kangaroos. They are attracted to the moving lights of night-time roadtrains.

The mammoth vehicle above is an Australian roadtrain, hauling a big load across the outback. Triple units are common. Sometimes, drivers (called "truckies") will be in charge of roadtrains with six or seven trailers.

Temperatures are sometimes so hot that truckies rest by day and drive by night. This conserves the tires, which wear away very quickly in the searing heat of the desert sun.

◁ This Leyland roadtrain glitters with chrome at a motor show. It comes complete with four shiny airhorns mounted on the cab.

Military trucks

Trucks used by the world's armed forces have lots of different jobs.

Canvas-topped trucks can carry troops and equipment. Larger vehicles can act as mobile command posts. Others can be the base unit for anti-aircraft missiles or they may haul massive cannon. Still larger vehicles, called TELs, are used as Transporter/Erector/Launchers to fire missiles.

▽ Tank transporters have drop-down ramps at the back. A powerful winch winds a steel cable to pull a tank on board. A tank like the one shown here weighs over 55 tons (50 mt).

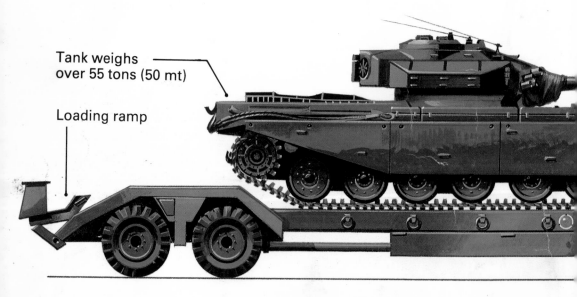

Tank weighs over 55 tons (50 mt)

Loading ramp

Construction engineers use military versions of road-building machinery to make emergency air bases or to build defensive earthworks.

Tank transporters come in especially useful to retrieve battle-damaged tanks which cannot move under their own power. Such tanks can be taken to safety behind the lines for repairs.

Military vehicles spend much time plowing through rough country, so they are built with a very high ground clearance where possible. Solid construction and armorplate are other military requirements.

△ This truck has a swing-over winch to sling its mobile command post load on to the ground.

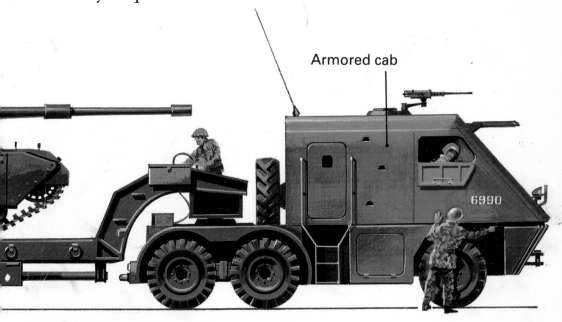

Armored cab

Dump trucks

△ At this highway building site, a front-end loader is used to fill dump trucks with soil.

Dump trucks are used to carry loads such as earth, sand and gravel.

Dump trucks are often found on construction sites where massive amounts of material have to be shifted. A popular method "on-site" is to use a front-end loader. When the truck has arrived at the dumping area, a hydraulic ram raises the loaded dump body and the tons of material slide out at the back.

▷ This Isuzu from Japan is a typical smaller-sized dump truck.

△ The GMC truck is a size up from the Isuzu. The metal load carrier is ribbed for strength.

Fire trucks

△ This fire truck can roar across ditches and plowed fields to reach a crashed aircraft. It comes with a powerful foam spray for quenching fierce fuel fires.

Fire trucks carry lots of heavy equipment. Ladders, pumps, hoses and firemen all have to be carried. For this reason fire trucks have powerful engines for rapid acceleration.

Water is used on many fires. Nearly 1,320 gallons (6,000 l) can be pumped every minute by a fire truck.

Fires on crashed aircraft usually involve fuel from the wing tanks. Fuel fires are sprayed with foam. Fuel floats on water, so the flames spread more quickly if water is used.

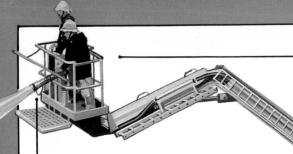

The platform has room for up to seven people. They can be rescued from many floors up.

Water is pumped through this nozzle.

Hydraulic rams push firefighting platform high in the air.

▷ This Simon fire truck is typical of the sort used by many city fire departments. Extending legs provide firm support when the platform is extended.

Trucks of tomorrow

▽ This future truck design has a streamlined cab, covers over the rear wheels and a close-coupled trailer. All these details smooth the airflow reducing the energy needed to move the truck along.

Many people complain about today's huge trucks. The noise, vibration and pollution they produce cause problems for the environment. Truck owners want better fuel consumption to reduce their running costs.

Future truck designs should

improve things. Carefully designed cabs, shaped in a wind tunnel, already reduce fuel consumption. It takes less energy to push a smooth body through the air than a square one. Future trucks are likely to be very smooth and streamlined in appearance.

New engine designs reduce noise, pollution and fuel consumption. Strict noise and pollution laws make things even better.

Vibration from heavy trucks is a difficult problem. Probably the best solution is to build more bypasses that stay out of cities.

△ This truck is based on the ideas of designer Luigi Colani. It has a "goldfish bowl" canopy to give the driver a view from all directions.

The trucking story

Early trucks were little more than motorized carts. Then came weather protection for the driver and covered areas for the load. Next came articulated vehicles and container trucks.

▽ This 1914 Fiat, from Italy, was a successful design. It had a canvas-covered cab.

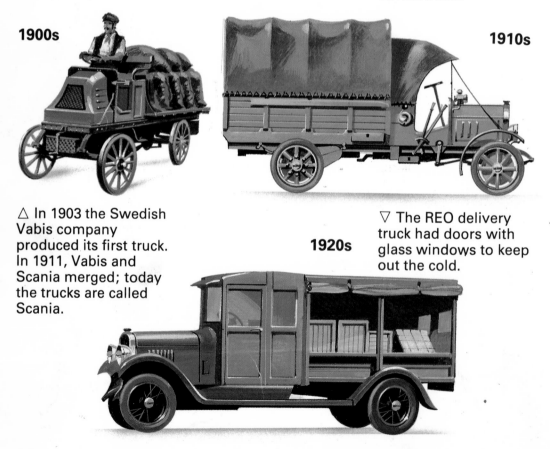

1900s

1910s

△ In 1903 the Swedish Vabis company produced its first truck. In 1911, Vabis and Scania merged; today the trucks are called Scania.

1920s

▽ The REO delivery truck had doors with glass windows to keep out the cold.

1930s

◁ This Ford tanker is one of the early articulated vehicles.

▽ The wide-look Dodge was a typical design for the time. It is hauling a container load.

1940s

1950s

△ The smooth-looking Kenworth came with a sleeper compartment.

▽ This slab-fronted Atkinson is pulling 21.5 tons (19 mt) of salt.

▷ The Unic was specially built for long distance trans-continental trucking.

1970s

1960s

Supertrucks

△ Racing neck-and-neck, a MAN from Germany and a British Scammel thunder along at over 80 mph (130 km/h). Truck racing attacts many star names, including Barry Sheene, better known for motorcycle racing.

Truck racing is becoming popular with truckers everywhere. The big rigs seem very ungainly as they roar around corners, but they are more stable than they look. Most of a truck's weight is on the bottom, with the engine, running gear and chassis.

A trucking Grand Prix has attractions besides the racing. Features may include jet-powered trucks, side shows and booths that sell trucking clothes, models, posters and other items.

Glossary

This list explains many of the technical words in this book.

Airhorn
Loud horn, operated by a blast of compressed air, like a mechanized trumpet. Chrome-plated airhorns are often mounted on cab roofs as decorations.

Articulated vehicle
One with two halves, a tractor and trailer.

Bypass
Road specially built to go around a congested city, town or village.

Cab-over
Word to describe trucks with a cab over the engine. Trucks like this are also known as forward control, because the driving position is ahead of the engine. A conventional, normal control, truck has the engine up front, under the hood.

Container
Standard-size metal box, used in international freight traffic. Can be transported by road, rail or sea. Smaller containers are carried in the freight holds of airliners.

Customized
Describes vehicles which have been modified in some way. This means just adding a shiny set of airhorns or a complete glossy paint job.

Diesel
Type of engine which uses diesel oil as its fuel. More economical than the same sized gas engine.

Frame
Strong metal backbone of a truck. Engine, cap, fuel tanks and running gear are all attached to the frame.

Rig
Slang word for a truck.

Rigid
Used to describe a non-articulated truck.

Roadtrain
Truck pulling three or more trailers. Much used in Australia.

Sleeper cab
Separate section behind the driving position where a trucker can rest and sleep.

Tachograph
Device in the cab which records the speed of a truck and the times it is driven. These are recorded on a paper disc. If speed limits or driving times have been exceeded, the tachograph records the facts.

Tractor
The pulling part of an articulated rig.

31

Index